NORTH BRIDGE HOUSE SENIOR SCHOOL

This book has been awarded to

Max Nedeljkovic-Gibbon

Academic Award

Geography

Manes

6.6.17

WHY? ENCYCLOPEDIA

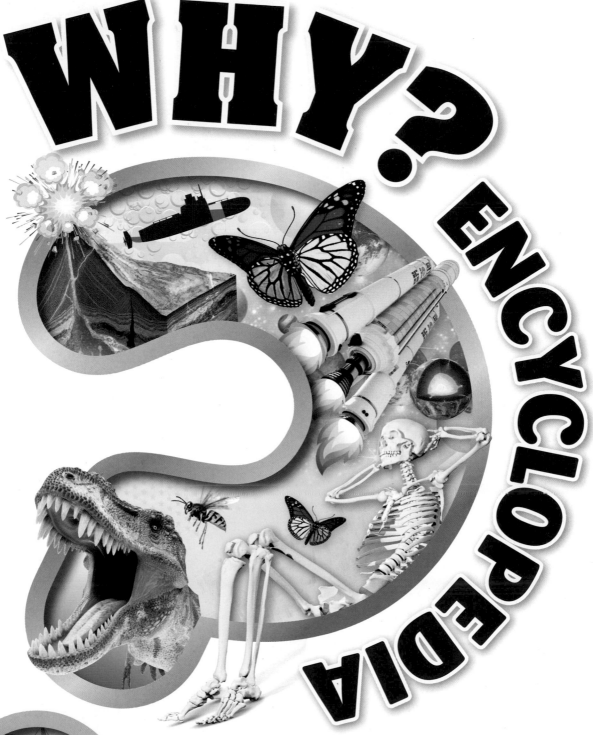

Brilliant answers to baffling questions

**LONDON, NEW YORK,
MELBOURNE, MUNICH, and DELHI**

Senior Editor Fleur Star
Editorial team Caroline Bingham, Annabel Blackledge, Rod Green,
Rob Houston, Ashwin Khurana, Susan Reuben, Jane Yorke
Senior Art Editor Spencer Holbrook
Design team Dave Ball, Steve Crozier, Carol Davis, Paul Drislane,
Rachael Grady, Samantha Richiardi, Steve Woosnam-Savage
Illustrators Adam Benton, Peter Bull,
Stuart Jackson-Carter, Arran Lewis
Photoshop retouching Steve Crozier
Cartography Simon Mumford
Consultants Dr Jacqueline Mitton (Space), Douglas Palmer (Earth),
Dr Kim Dennis-Bryan (Living World), Philip Parker (History),
Ian Graham (Science), Dr Penny Preston (Human Body)

Jacket Editor Maud Whatley
Jacket Designer Laura Brim
Jacket Design Development Manager Sophia MTT
Picture Research Sumedha Chopra

Producer, Pre-production Francesca Wardell
Senior producer Mandy Inness

Managing Editor Gareth Jones
Managing Art Editor Philip Letsu
Publisher Andrew Macintyre
Publishing Director Jonathan Metcalf
Associate Publishing Director Liz Wheeler
Art Director Phil Ormerod

First published in Great Britain in 2014
by Dorling Kindersley Limited,
80 Strand, London WC2R 0RL

Copyright © 2014 Dorling Kindersley Limited

A Penguin Random House Company

10 9 8 7 6
020–192382–Aug/2014

A CIP catalogue record for this book
is available from the British Library.

ISBN: 978-1-4093-5207-5

Printed and bound in China by Hung Hing

Discover more at www.dk.com

CONTENTS

SPACE

THE EARTH

LIVING WORLD

HISTORY

SCIENCE

HUMAN BODY

Space

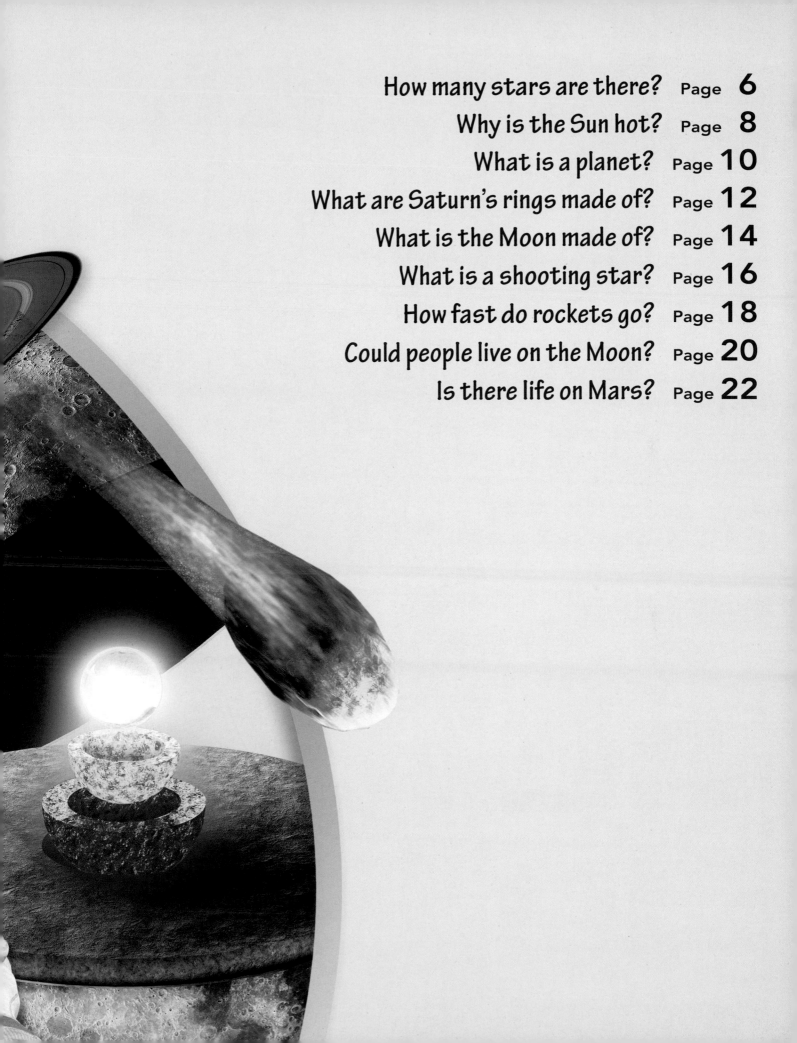

How many stars are there?

Our galaxy, called the Milky Way, has hundreds of billions of stars. There are trillions more galaxies in the Universe, each containing countless stars. From the Earth, the Milky Way looks like a band of light in the night sky. If you could fly above our galaxy, it would look like a glittering wheel.

Galaxy shapes

The shape of the Milky Way is called a barred spiral – it has a bar across its centre that connects the spiral arms. Galaxies come in different shapes, such as these below.

Spiral

Lenticular

Elliptical

Irregular

3 Gas clouds

⭐ Centre of the galaxy

A black hole lies hidden in the centre of our galaxy. It is called a "black" hole because nothing can escape this point, not even light.

The biggest stars are called supergiants.

olar System 2

The oldest known star is thought to be **13.2 billion years old.**

1 Centre of galaxy

5 Dust clouds

5 Dust clouds
The dark areas between the spiral arms are clouds of dust. These are called nebulae.

4 Spiral arm

4 Spiral arm
Our galaxy is a spiral shape with four major "arms". Stars, gas, and dust are found in these arms.

2 Solar System
Our Solar System contains eight planets, around 170 moons, and millions of asteroids and comets. They all orbit (travel around) the star we call the Sun.

3 Gas clouds
Our galaxy contains huge clouds of gas. Stars form in the gas clouds, lighting them up.

Quick quiz

 What is the name of our galaxy?

 What is in the centre of the galaxy?

 What is the age of the oldest known star?

Why is the Sun hot?

The Sun is a giant ball of different gases. In the Sun's centre, which is called the core, these gases produce energy in the form of heat and light. This makes the Sun hot and bright. The energy then travels out through space, reaching Earth in just 8 minutes.

Spots on the Sun

Dark patches on the Sun's surface are called sunspots. They are the cooler parts of the surface, but are still incredibly hot.

Solar eclipse

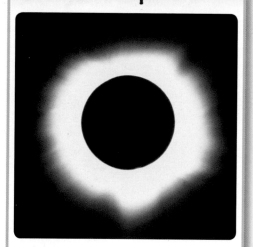

A total solar eclipse happens when the Moon comes between the Earth and the Sun, blocking it from view. The sky goes dark and we can see the glowing atmosphere around the Sun called the corona.

Hot gas

The Sun is not solid. It is mostly a mixture of two gases called hydrogen and helium.

You could fit about **1 million Earths** inside the **Sun.**

Swirling loops

Gigantic loops of glowing gas shoot out from the surface of the Sun into space. They can last for months.

In the centre

The centre, or core, is the hottest part of the Sun. This is where the gases produce energy. The energy takes 100,000 years to reach the Sun's surface.

The temperature at the Sun's core is 15 million °C (27 million °F).

Sizzling surface

Bubbles of hot gas make the Sun's surface appear grainy. You should never look at the Sun, though. Its light is so bright, it can damage your eyes.

What is a planet?

A planet is a ball-shaped object that orbits (travels around) a star. Eight planets orbit the star we call the Sun. The four planets nearest the Sun are small and rocky. The four outer planets are larger and made mostly of gas. Together, the Sun and the eight planets make up the Solar System.

Quick quiz

 Is Venus bigger or smaller than Earth?

 Why does Mars look red?

 How strong are the winds on Neptune?

The Sun
The Sun is a star at the centre of the Solar System. Every planet orbits (travels around) it.

Giant Jupiter
Jupiter is the biggest planet – larger than the other seven planets put together.

A day on Jupiter is

Mini Mercury
Mercury is the smallest planet and the closest one to the Sun.

Life on Earth
Earth is where we live. It is the only planet in the Solar System known to have life.

Spinning backwards
Venus is slightly smaller than Earth. It spins in the opposite direction to most of the other planets.

The red planet
Mars is known as the red planet. Its colour comes from the iron minerals in the soil on its surface.

Moving around the Sun

Each planet travels around the Sun on its own path, or orbit. The length of time it takes to make one orbit is called a year. Planets also spin as they orbit. The time it takes to make one complete spin is called a day.

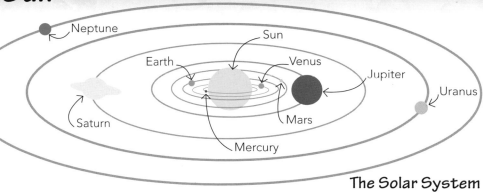

The Solar System

The ringed planet

Saturn is surrounded by visible rings, which are made up of billions of chunks of ice.

Mercury takes **88 days** to travel around the Sun, but **Neptune** takes **164 years!**

10 hours long.

Tilted to the Sun

Uranus is tilted so that its north pole (the top of most planets) is at its side.

Windy Neptune

The winds on Neptune can be nine times stronger than those on Earth.

What are Saturn's rings made of?

The rings of Saturn are made up of billions of pieces of ice. Some are tiny, while others are the size of a house. No one knows how they formed.

Saturn is about 750 times bigger than the Earth.

How many rings?

Saturn has seven main rings around it, along with at least 10 more narrow rings.

Many moons

Scientists have discovered 62 moons orbiting Saturn, and there may be even more. The biggest is called Titan – it is even bigger than the planet Mercury.

Around the middle

The objects in the rings all orbit (travel around) the middle of the planet (its equator).

Squashed shape

Saturn is not a perfect ball-shape. It has a squashed top and bottom, and bulges in the middle.

Mind the gap

The two widest rings are named A and B, and are the wide grey rings here. They are separated by a gap.

A

B

A **day** on Saturn lasts just **10.5 hours**, but its **year** is longer than **29 Earth years.**

Quick quiz

 How many main rings does Saturn have?

 What is the name of Saturn's largest moon?

 What are Saturn's two widest rings called?

What is the Moon made of?

The Moon is made of a mixture of rocks and metals. About 4.5 billion years ago, a small planet smashed into the Earth. Lots of chunks broke off and blasted into space. The Moon was made when some of these joined together again.

Solid rock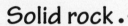

The mantle is a layer that starts 50 km (31 miles) below the Moon's surface. It is made mainly of solid rock.

Walking on the Moon

The Moon is the only place apart from the Earth where human beings have walked. From 1969 to 1972, a total of 12 astronauts landed on the Moon. They did experiments, took photographs, and brought back samples of rock. This picture is from the very first Moon landing in 1969.

Cratered crust

The Moon's outside, or crust, is made of hard rock. Its surface is covered in very fine, grey dust, and is also scarred with craters. These were made by asteroids that crashed into the Moon during its early life.

Solid iron
The Moon's inner core is a massive ball of hot, solid iron.

Every year, the **Moon** moves 4 cm (1.5 in) further away from the Earth.

Liquid iron
The outer core surrounds the inner core. It is made from hot, liquid iron.

Melting mantle
The inner mantle is partly melted, so some of it is solid and some of it is liquid.

Quick quiz

 How old is the Moon?

 How many people have landed on the Moon?

 Is the centre of the Moon liquid or solid?

What is a shooting star?

A shooting star looks like a fast streak of light in the night sky, lasting for just a second. Also called a meteor, it is not a star, but a small piece of rock or metal that burns up as it enters the Earth's atmosphere.

Millions of meteors enter the Earth's atmosphere every day.

Fading fast...
A meteor's trail fades quickly because the meteor moves very fast – about 70 km (45 miles) per second.

Blazing a trail...
A trail of light follows the meteor. As it travels, it rubs up against the gas in the atmosphere, making the gas glow.

The Hoba meteorite

Most meteors burn up in the atmosphere, but when one lands on Earth it is called a meteorite. The largest intact meteorite ever found weighs 60 tonnes (66 tons). It was discovered in Hoba West farm, Namibia, Africa.

Quick quiz

⭐ What is another word for a shooting star?

⭐ How heavy is the Hoba meteorite?

⭐ What is a very bright shooting star called?

Incredibly bright shooting stars are called **fireballs**.

Space fragment

Most meteors are very small. They range in size from a pebble down to a grain of sand.

Could people live on the Moon?

There is no air, food, or water on the Moon, so it would be very difficult to live there. When astronauts first walked on the Moon more than 45 years ago, they wore special suits to keep them alive.

Heated hands.
The astronaut's gloves had heaters in the fingers because it could get extremely cold on the Moon.

Moon camp

Some people believe that we might be living on the Moon in just 20 years' time, perhaps in a base that looks like the one below. It would have supplies of air, water, and food.

Drilling deep.
Astronauts drilled holes in the Moon to put in detectors and to dig up rock samples.

Moon boots.
The astronauts' boots were strong to cope with the Moon's rocky surface, which could also get very hot.

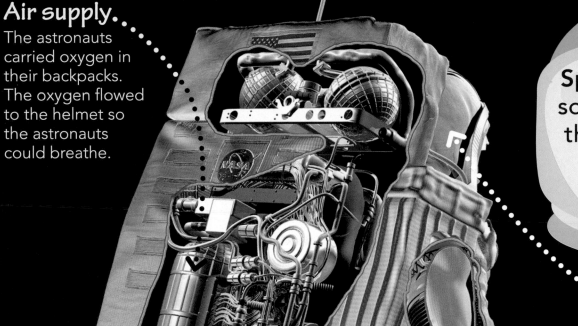

Air supply
The astronauts carried oxygen in their backpacks. The oxygen flowed to the helmet so the astronauts could breathe.

Space suits are so complicated, they take **over an hour** to put on.

Sun shade
As well as helping the astronauts to breathe, the helmet protected their eyes from the blinding glare of the Sun.

Keeping cool
The space suit had water running through tubes, under the fabric. This made sure the astronauts did not get too hot.

Pressure suit
Astronauts wore a tight rubber suit, called a pressure garment. It had joints so they could move more easily.

Quick quiz

 Why do Moon boots have to be strong?

 How did astronauts breathe on the Moon?

 How long does it take to put on a space suit?

Is there life on Mars?

No life has been found on Mars. However, life might have existed long ago if the conditions were right. A robot called Curiosity has been sent to study the planet to find out if it was warmer and wetter in the past.

Sending signals
There are three antennae on Curiosity. Scientists on Earth use them to communicate with the robot.

Curiosity's top speed is **180 metres per hour** (0.1 mph). That is about the **speed** of a **tortoise!**

Taking pictures

Curiosity has 17 cameras, which allow scientists on Earth to see whatever it can see. It also has a laser that can turn rocks to dust to find out what they are made of.

Curiosity took more than 8 months to reach Mars.

Working hard

Curiosity's robotic hand has lots of tools. Here it is using a tool to scrape away the surface rock.

On the move

The rover has six tough wheels that help it to travel across the bumpy surface.

Quick quiz

 Have we discovered life on Mars?

 What are Curiosity's antennae for?

 How many cameras does Curiosity have?

The Earth

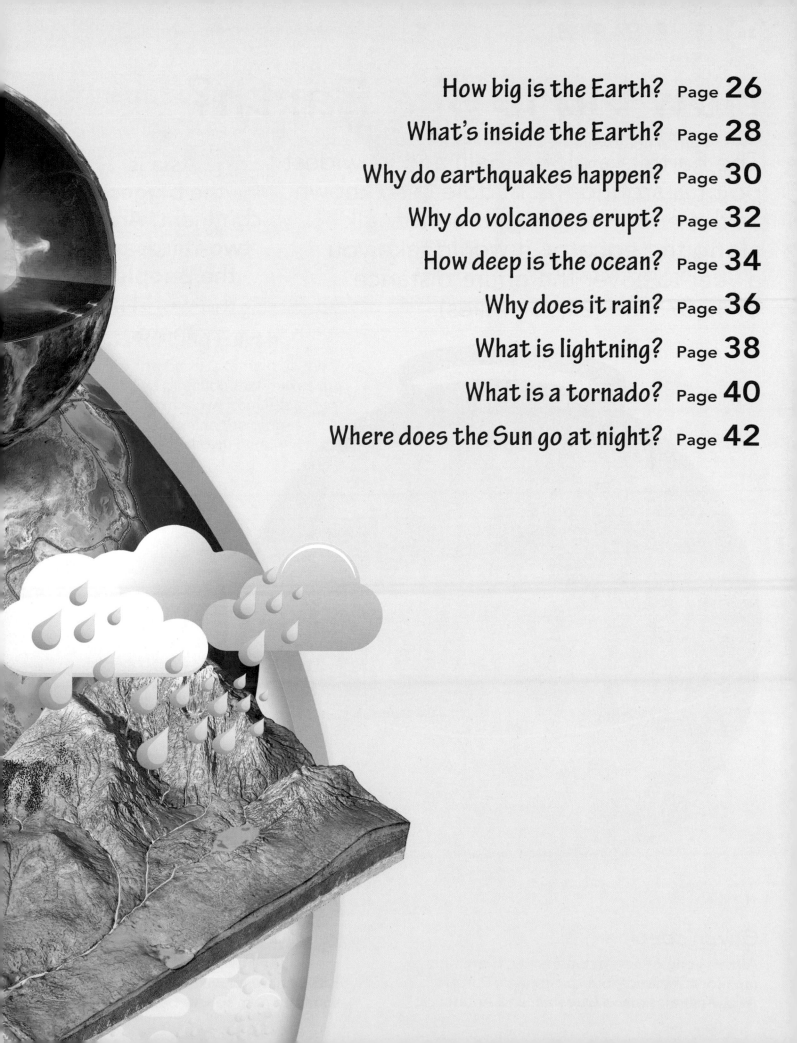

Outside the Earth

The Earth is surrounded by layers of gases, called the atmosphere. These protect the planet from the Sun's rays, and give us the air we need to breathe.

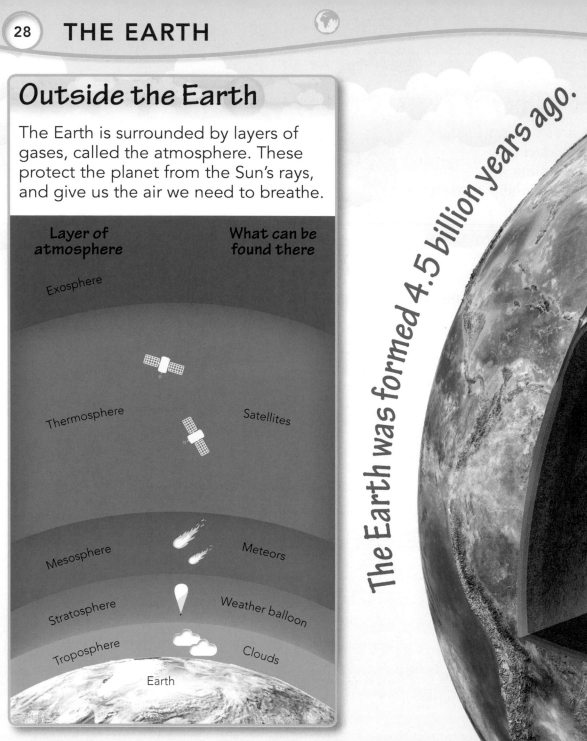

Layer of atmosphere	What can be found there
Exosphere	
Thermosphere	Satellites
Mesosphere	Meteors
Stratosphere	Weather balloon
Troposphere	Clouds
Earth	

The Earth was formed 4.5 billion years ago.

What's inside the Earth?

The planet Earth is a giant rocky ball spinning in space. We live on its thin outer layer, called the crust, but there are more layers on the inside. At the very centre is a hot, solid, metal core.

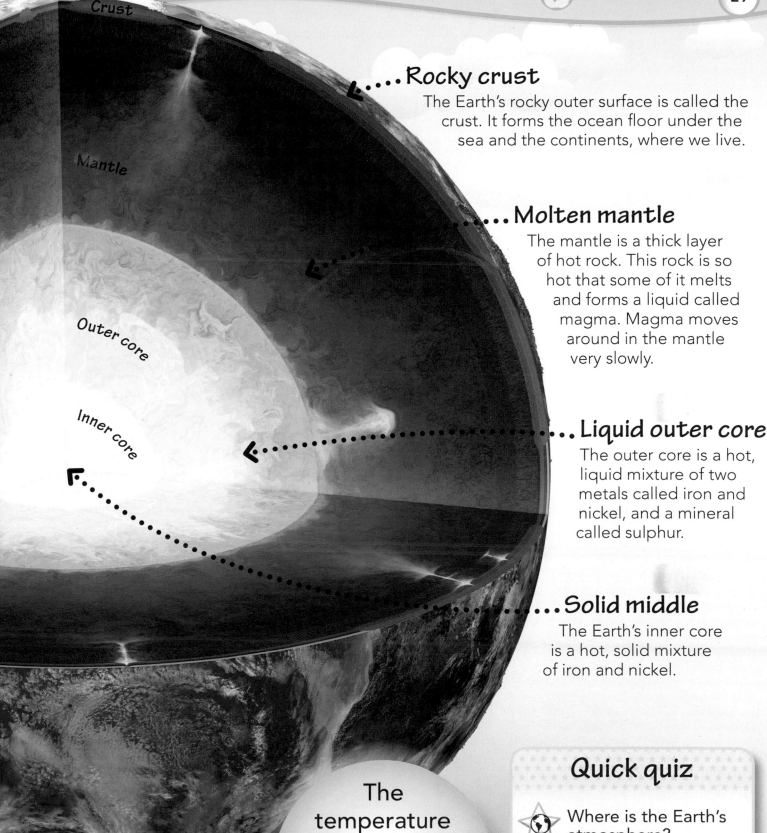

Crust

Mantle

Outer core

Inner core

Rocky crust
The Earth's rocky outer surface is called the crust. It forms the ocean floor under the sea and the continents, where we live.

Molten mantle
The mantle is a thick layer of hot rock. This rock is so hot that some of it melts and forms a liquid called magma. Magma moves around in the mantle very slowly.

Liquid outer core
The outer core is a hot, liquid mixture of two metals called iron and nickel, and a mineral called sulphur.

Solid middle
The Earth's inner core is a hot, solid mixture of iron and nickel.

The temperature of the **Earth's inner core** is **6,000 °C (10,800 °F)**.

Quick quiz

 Where is the Earth's atmosphere?

 What do we call the Earth's outer layer?

 Which layer is made of hot, solid metal?

Why do earthquakes happen?

The Earth's crust is like a huge jigsaw puzzle, made up of pieces called plates. These plates are moving very slowly, all the time. When two plates rub against each other, the pressure can cause earthquakes, making the ground shake.

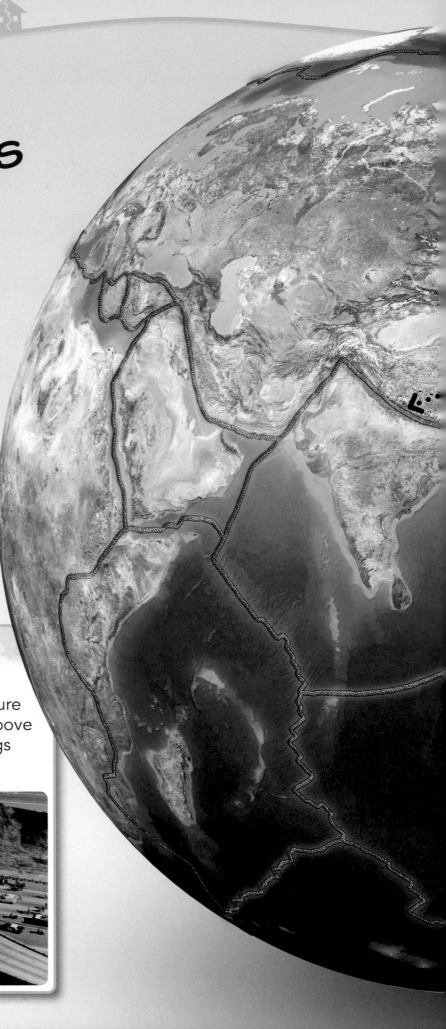

Earthquake power

Earthquakes can be measured on the Richter scale. Weak earthquakes measure less than 3.5 on the scale, but those above 7 are strong enough to topple buildings and make roads and bridges collapse.

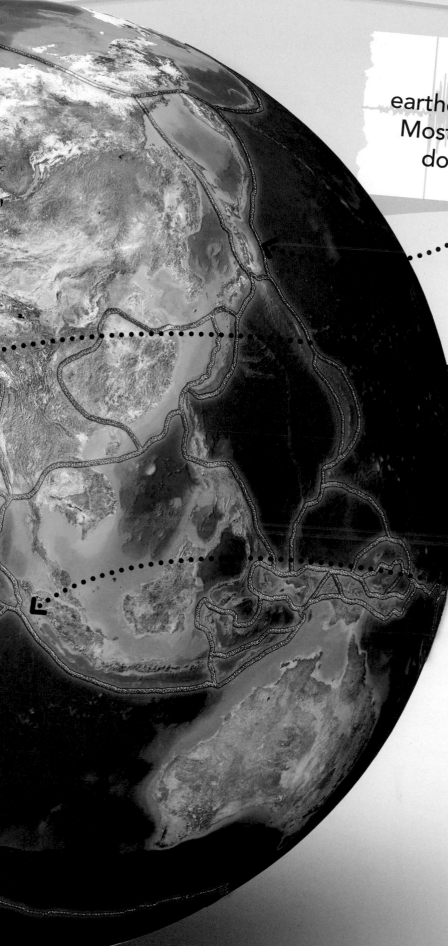

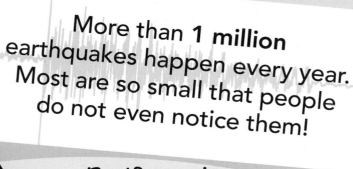

More than **1 million** earthquakes happen every year. Most are so small that people do not even notice them!

Pacific quake

In 2011, a huge earthquake took place in Japan. It began in the Pacific Ocean, where one plate moved beneath another.

Making mountains

The Himalayas formed when two plates pushed together, making the ground rise up into huge mountains. These plates are still moving against each other, which often causes earthquakes in this region.

Giant waves

In 2004, an earthquake under the Indian Ocean caused a tsunami – an enormous wave. The waves washed ashore and caused destruction in 14 different countries.

Quick quiz

 What causes earthquakes?

 How are earthquakes measured?

 How many earthquakes happen each year?

Why do volcanoes erupt?

Volcanoes can erupt when pressure deep underground forces hot, liquid rock (called magma) from inside the Earth up to the surface. An eruption blasts out clouds of ash and molten (melted) rock into the air around it.

Escape route
Magma rises up a main pipe from deep within the Earth's crust and is forced towards the surface.

Trapped underground
Pools of magma build up deep underground. This hot, liquid rock comes from the Earth's interior.

Quick quiz

- Where does magma come from?
- Why are volcanoes often cone shaped?
- How many volcanoes erupt each year?

Ash clouds

Thick clouds of burning hot ash are blasted up to several kilometres into the Earth's atmosphere.

Rivers of fire

An erupting volcano can produce fountains of red hot lava that run down its sides, burning everything in their path. When an eruption blows off the top of the volcano, lava may also form a lake in the crater that is left behind.

Flowing lava

At the Earth's surface, magma is called lava, which flows down the sides of the volcano. The lava cools in layers, often with ash in between, that give the volcano its cone shape.

Around 50–70 **volcanoes** erupt in the world each year and about **20 volcanoes** are erupting right now.

The temperature of lava is a scorching 1,000 °C (1,800 °F).

How deep is the ocean?

The deepest part of the ocean is 11 km (7 miles) under water. Just like on dry land, the ocean floor has mountains and valleys. The deepest parts are called trenches. Not much lives at these cold, dark depths, but there is much more life in the zones above.

0 m (0 ft)   200 m (660 ft)   1,000 m (3,300 ft)

Corals
Sponges
Starfish
Seaweeds
Scuba diver
Mackerel
Jellyfish
Bluntnose sixgill shark
Sponges   Comb jelly
Whale shark
Tuna
Sperm whale
Squid

Sunlit sea

The top zone is the sunlit zone, where sunlight reaches 200 m (660 ft) down into the clear, blue water. Most sea life lives here, where there is plenty of food. Scuba divers can safely explore to depths of around 50 m (165 ft).

Murky twilight

The next level, down to 1,000 m (3,300 ft), is called the twilight zone. Fewer fish and sea creatures live here, where the sea is darker and colder.

Dark waters

The dark zone drops from 1,000 m to 4,000 m (3,300 ft to 13,100 ft). Only deep-sea fish and animals can survive in these cold waters, where there is less chance of finding food.

4,000 m
(13,100 ft)

11,000 m
(36,000 ft)

Deep-sea anglerfish

Hagfish

Black swallower

Cusk eel

Submarine

The cusk eel is the world's deepest living fish, surviving at 8,000 m (26,200 ft) below the surface.

Deepest depths

Little is known about the deepest, darkest areas of the ocean, which stretch down to almost 11,000 m (36,000 ft). These are zones that we are only just beginning to explore for signs of life.

Chimneys under the sea

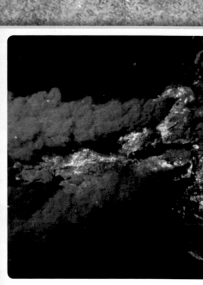

Water heated by hot rocks can spring out of the sea bed through large cracks in the Earth's crust. Grains of minerals in the water make it look like smoke. The grains pile up and quickly harden into chimney-like towers up to 60 m (200 ft) high.

Why does it rain?

The clouds in the sky are made up of tiny water droplets, which rise into the air when the Sun heats the sea. The droplets get larger and heavier, then fall to the ground as rain. This water runs into rivers, which flow from the land back to the sea. This never-ending journey is called the water cycle.

2 Drifting clouds

Winds blow the clouds over the land. When the clouds drift into cooler air, the tiny water droplets start to join together to form larger, heavier raindrops.

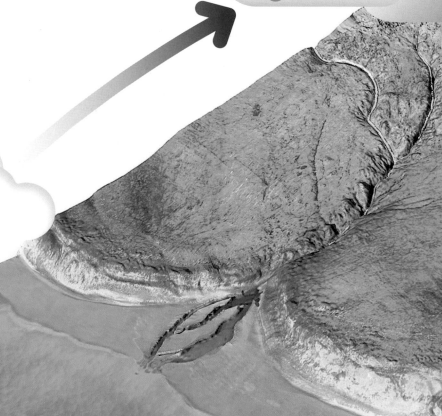

1 Rising water

The Sun heats the sea and turns the water into invisible water vapour, which rises into the air. The warm water vapour cools into millions of tiny water droplets, which form clouds.

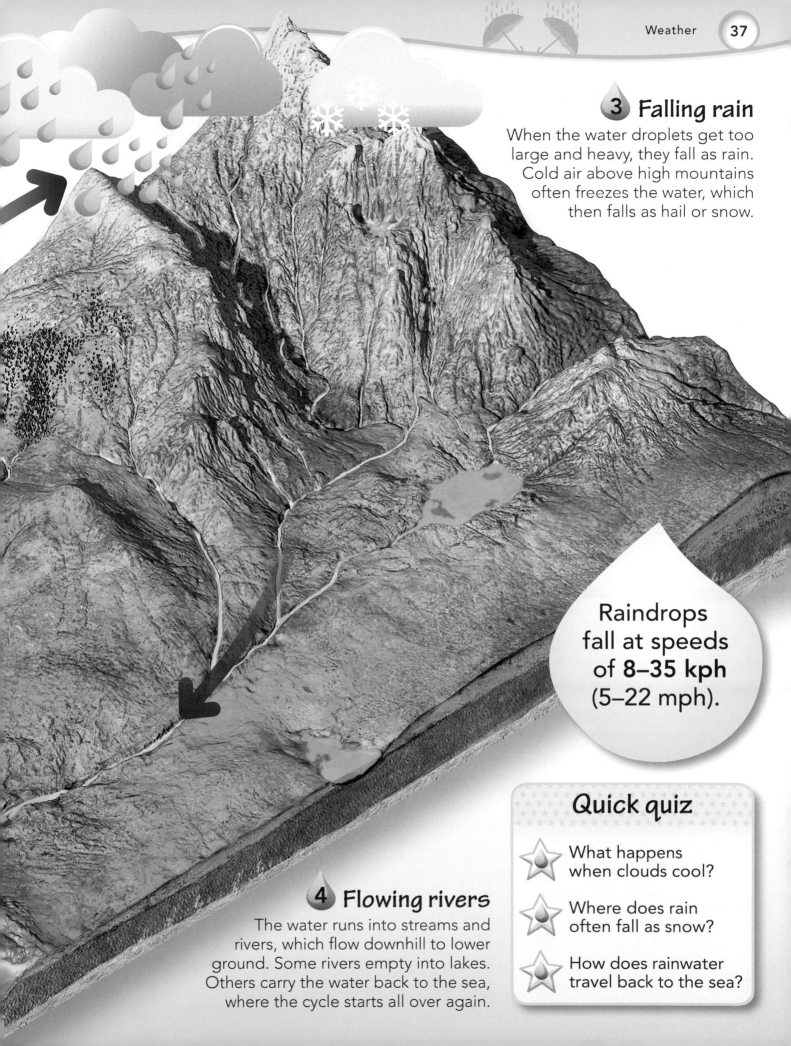

3 Falling rain

When the water droplets get too large and heavy, they fall as rain. Cold air above high mountains often freezes the water, which then falls as hail or snow.

Raindrops fall at speeds of **8–35 kph** (5–22 mph).

4 Flowing rivers

The water runs into streams and rivers, which flow downhill to lower ground. Some rivers empty into lakes. Others carry the water back to the sea, where the cycle starts all over again.

Quick quiz

★ What happens when clouds cool?

★ Where does rain often fall as snow?

★ How does rainwater travel back to the sea?

What is lightning?

Lightning is a bright flash of electricity produced by some powerful storms. This happens when the raindrops in clouds turn to ice and knock together, creating electricity. When too much of this electricity builds up, it is released in the form of giant sparks called lightning.

Super storms

Thunderstorms are made up of several storm clouds joined together. They can stretch as wide as 30 km (19 miles) across.

Noisy flash

A flash of lightning is burning hot. It heats up the air, which expands very quickly and produces a noisy crash of thunder. You see the lightning before you hear the thunder because light travels faster than sound.

Lightning flashes are a scorching **30,000°C (54,000°F) – five times hotter** than the surface of the Sun.

Fearsome forks

Forked lighting is the name for lightning that appears as jagged lines of light split into several branches.

Ground strikes

Cloud-to-ground lightning strikes tall things, such as trees and buildings. The powerful electric current can cause great damage and set things on fire.

Lightning strikes last a fraction of a second.

Sparking clouds

Not all lightning strikes reach the ground. Cloud-to-cloud lightning happens when huge sparks of electricity leap across the sky from one storm cloud to another. These huge flashes of light are known as sheet lightning.

Quick quiz

How hot is a flash of lightning?

Why does lightning create thunder?

What is sheet lightning?

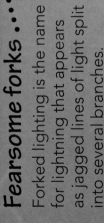

What is a tornado?

Tornadoes are powerful, swirling, spinning winds that sometimes form beneath a storm cloud. Wherever they touch land, tornadoes sweep across the ground, leaving behind a trail of destruction. A tornado can last for just a few seconds or more than an hour.

2 Spinning air

As warm air meets cool, swirling air high in the cloud, it starts to spin. Soon the air lower down is spinning, too.

Whirling water

When a whirling air mass passes over warm, shallow seas, it sucks up water into a funnel of air that is called a waterspout. A waterspout may have lower wind speeds than a tornado, but it can last far longer.

3 Cloud column

More of the surrounding air is pulled in and the growing tornado spins even faster. It then forms a column of twisting cloud that reaches the ground.

1 Stormy weather

Dark, violent storm clouds build up where warm, moist air rising from the land meets cool, dry air in the sky.

Around **1,000 tornadoes** a year strike in the United States, mostly in an area called **Tornado Alley.**

Tornadoes spin at speeds of up to 320 kph (200 mph).

4 Blown away

The strong, whirling winds suck up and destroy anything lying in their path. A tornado can tear up trees, buildings, and cars, then drop them many kilometres away when it has weakened.

Quick quiz

 How long can tornadoes last?

 What is a waterspout?

 How fast do tornadoes spin?

Living world

Are plants alive?

Just like animals, plants are living things: they are able to grow, reproduce (have babies), and die. Plants are just one of five main groups, or kingdoms, of living things in the world.

Maritime pine trees

Smallest living things

Bacteria are too small to see without a microscope. They are made up of just one cell – the tiny building blocks that all living things are made from. People have trillions of cells.

Fly agaric

Pink waxcap

Protists

Bacteria

Sulphur tuft

Hare's ear

Lichen

Devil's matchstick

Single cells

Another group of tiny living things live in water or in soil. Some make food like plants; others take in food like animals.

Fungi

Mushrooms and toadstools are part of the group called fungi. They feed on dead plants and animals.

Asian elephant

African fish eagle

Saltwater crocodile

Parrotfish

Black tree fern

Goliath bird-eating spider

Oxeye daisy

Animals

All animals eat other living things for energy. Whether they run, crawl, swim, or fly, most animals must move around to find the food they need to survive.

Plants

Nearly all plants stay in one place, rooted to the same spot. Most plants use sunlight, water, air, and their green leaves to make their own food.

There are around **289,000 different kinds of plants** living in the world.

Quick quiz

 How many cells are bacteria made up of?

 What do most plants use to make food?

 What do animals eat for energy?

Why are leaves green?

Leaves are green because they contain a green chemical called chlorophyll. Plants use chlorophyll to absorb sunlight so they can make food. This process is called photosynthesis. Photosynthesis takes place during the day when the Sun is out.

Sunlight

Sunlight

Carbon dioxide

Carbon dioxide in

During the day, leaves take in carbon dioxide from the air, water from the tree's roots, and sunlight. They mix them together to make sugar and oxygen.

Oxygen

Oxygen out

The leaves release the oxygen they have made, because they do not need it, and store the sugar for food.

Quick quiz

 What is photosynthesis?

 What does a tree's roots take in?

 Why does a tree take in oxygen?

Spreading out
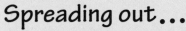

A tree's roots may reach deep down or spread far and wide to gather as much water as possible.

Losing water

The surface of a leaf has tiny openings, called stomata. They open to let gases in and out, and water escapes as a gas called water vapour. More water flows to the leaf to replace the water vapour. This keeps water flowing through the whole plant.

Stomata

Cells

Water vapour

Oxygen

3 Oxygen in

Plants absorb oxygen at night. They use it to turn the food they have made during the day into energy.

4 Carbon dioxide out

At night, plants release carbon dioxide because they do not need it to make food.

Carbon dioxide

Watery roots

Trees absorb (take in) water from the soil through their roots. The water travels up the trunk to the branches and leaves.

The food that plants make is a kind of **sugar** called **glucose**.

Why do plants have flowers?

A plant's flowers help it to reproduce (make more plants). Flowers attract insects and some birds and bats. These animals carry a grainy dust called pollen from one flower to another. Flowers use this pollen to produce seeds.

Spreading seeds

A plant needs to spread its seeds so that new plants can grow. Many plants make seeds inside fruit. Animals eat the fruit and scatter these seeds in their poo. Some other flowers, such as dandelions, produce very light seeds that blow away on the wind.

Sticky stigma
Visiting insects may rub against the stigma, leaving pollen grains behind. Each grain grows a tube that travels down the style to the ovary.

Stigma

Style

Anther

Pollen store
Anthers produce the tiny grains of pollen that stick to visiting insects.

Pretty petals
The colour, shape, and size of a flower's petals, and the smell of the flower, attracts insects.

Anther

Anther

Collecting pollen

Insects such as bees visit flowers to drink nectar and collect pollen. As they crawl on the flower, some pollen grains from the anthers stick to their bodies and legs. When the bees visit other flowers, this pollen rubs off on their stigmas.

Pollen

Sweet food

Nectar is made at the bottom of the flower. Insects crawl inside to reach the sweet, sugary liquid.

The Queen of the Andes is a South American plant that flowers after 80–150 years and then dies.

Ovary

Inside the flower

The ovary contains the plant's eggs. Pollen that collects on the stigma comes down the style to join with the eggs and grow into seeds.

Quick quiz

 Which part of a flower produces the pollen?

 Why do insects visit flowers?

 Where is nectar made?

How many animals are there in the world?

There are trillions of individual animals living in the world – far too many to count! However, scientists think there are about 8.7 million different species (kinds) of animals on the planet. They sort animal species with similar features into different groups.

Emu

Giant tortoise

Chameleon

Caecilian

Bottlenose dolphin

Giraffe

Macaw

Owl

Crocodile

Lion

Peafowl

King penguin

Green iguana

Swan

Hare

Scarlet ibis

Bald eagle

Grey wolf

Mammals

Red kangaroo

Chimpanzee

Birds

Mammals

Most mammals give birth to live young and all feed their babies on milk.

Birds

Birds have feathers and most of them can fly using their wings. They produce young by laying eggs.

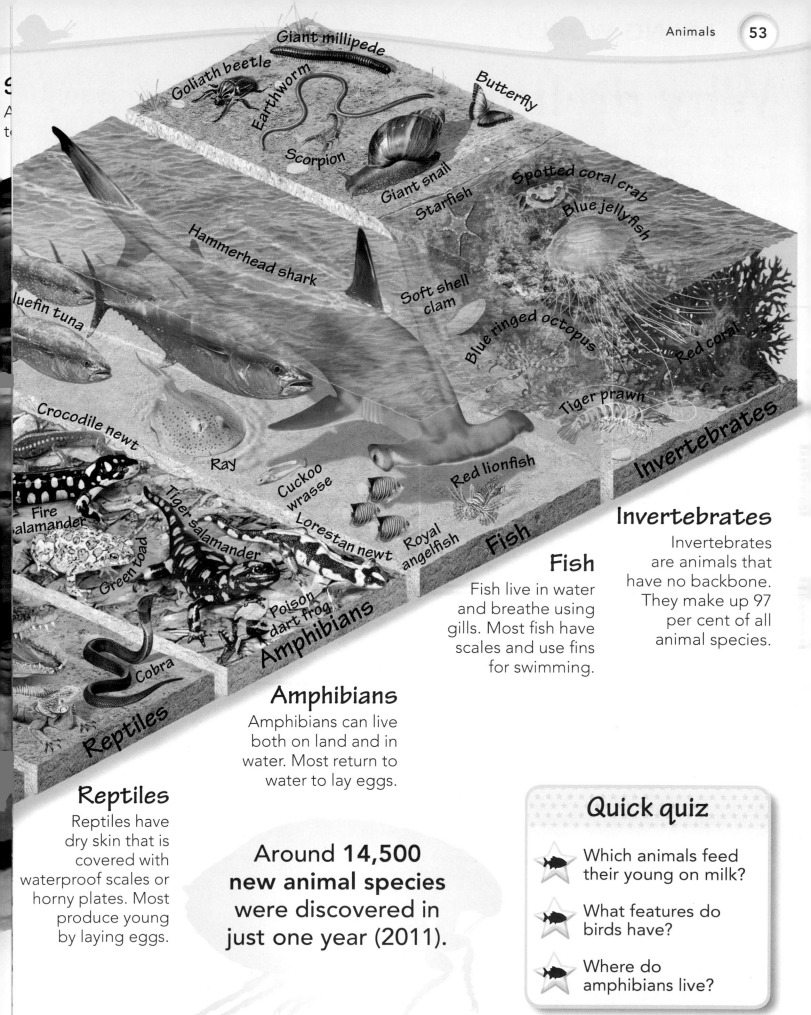

Giant millipede

Goliath beetle

Earthworm

Butterfly

Scorpion

Giant snail

Starfish

Spotted coral crab

Blue jellyfish

Hammerhead shark

Soft shell clam

Blue ringed octopus

Red coral

Bluefin tuna

Crocodile newt

Ray

Cuckoo wrasse

Tiger prawn

Fire salamander

Tiger salamander

Green toad

Lorestan newt

Red lionfish

Invertebrates

Poison dart frog

Royal angelfish

Cobra

Amphibians

Fish

Reptiles

Invertebrates

Invertebrates are animals that have no backbone. They make up 97 per cent of all animal species.

Fish

Fish live in water and breathe using gills. Most fish have scales and use fins for swimming.

Amphibians

Amphibians can live both on land and in water. Most return to water to lay eggs.

Reptiles

Reptiles have dry skin that is covered with waterproof scales or horny plates. Most produce young by laying eggs.

Around **14,500 new animal species** were discovered in **just one year (2011).**

Quick quiz

★ Which animals feed their young on milk?

★ What features do birds have?

★ Where do amphibians live?

How do tadpoles turn into frogs?

Tadpoles hatch from frog's eggs laid in water. As they grow, tadpoles slowly start to change shape. They grow legs and lose their tails as they develop into young frogs that can live on land. This change from tadpole to frog is called metamorphosis.

The goliath frog is the **largest in the world**. It can grow up to **32 cm (13 in) long**.

1. Hatching eggs

Female frogs lay jelly-like clumps of eggs called frogspawn in ponds and rivers. The eggs hatch into tiny, swimming tadpoles.

2. Living in water

Tadpoles spend their first weeks of life in water. They swim using their long tails and breathe using gills, like fish.

3. Growing legs

After two months, tadpoles grow two back legs. They start to feed a lot, nibbling on algae in the water.

Animal groups

Frogs, newts, and worm-like creatures called caecilians make up the three groups of animals called amphibians. Like frogs, the young of these animals hatch from eggs and look very different to the fully-grown adults.

Frog   Newt   Caecilian

5 Living on land

By four months, frogs are fully grown, with strong back legs, which help them to swim, climb, and leap on land. Adult frogs will return to the water to find a mate and lay eggs.

4 Breathing air

After three months, tadpoles grow lungs to breathe air from the surface of the water. They also grow front legs and their tails start to shrivel up.

Quick quiz

 Where do frogs lay their eggs?

 When do tadpoles grow back legs?

 When do tadpoles lose their tails?

How can fish breathe under water?

Living things have to breathe because they need oxygen to survive. People use their lungs to take in oxygen from the air, but fish have organs called gills at the sides of their heads, which allow them to get oxygen from the water.

More than **32,500 different kinds** of fish live in the world's **rivers, lakes,** and **oceans.**

1 Water flows in

When a fish opens its mouth, water rushes in and flows towards its gills.

Water in

Water out

Water out

2 Water filter

The water is pushed through bony spines inside the fish's head called gill rakers. These clean the water and stop sand or mud getting through.

3 Feathery filaments

The water then flows out of the fish's mouth through its gills, which contain feathery strands called filaments. These filaments take the oxygen from the water and pass it into the fish's blood.

Slippery scales

Most fish have a smooth body covered with scales. These help to protect the fish's body.

Fish first appeared on the Earth 500 million years ago.

Quick quiz

 Where are the gills on a fish's body?

 What do the feathery filaments do?

 Can sea mammals breathe under water?

Breathing through blowholes

Not all sea creatures breathe using gills. Whales are mammals with lungs and so they must swim to the surface to breathe air. Whales draw in air and blow it out through blowholes on the top of their heads.

What's the biggest spider?

The world's biggest spider is the goliath bird-eating tarantula. It is the heaviest spider at 175 g (6.2 oz), and with its legs stretched out, it is 28 cm (11 in) wide. This giant, hairy spider hunts at night, waiting to pounce on passing prey.

There are more than **42,000 different kinds** of spider.

Bristly body

The hair-like bristles on a tarantula's body are used to feel vibrations. This helps the tarantulas to sense things around them and also makes up for their poor eyesight.

Body case

All spiders have a hard, outer layer called an exoskeleton to protect them. As they get bigger, spiders wriggle out of their exoskeleton and grow a new one.

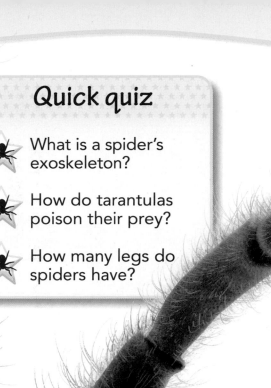

Quick quiz

★ What is a spider's exoskeleton?

★ How do tarantulas poison their prey?

★ How many legs do spiders have?

Gripping claws

Tarantulas have a pair of claws at the end of each leg, which they use to grip when climbing.

Catching prey

Many spiders trap flying insects by spinning a web made from strong silk threads. The spider then wraps its prey in sticky threads so that it can't move. Spiders can't eat solid food, so they inject their prey with special juices. These turn their meal into a liquid, which the spiders then suck up.

Bendy legs

All spiders have eight legs and each leg has six joints. This makes them very nimble.

Fearsome fangs

Tarantulas have two large fangs that inject venom (poison) into their prey. They feed mainly on insects, but also eat mice, frogs, small lizards, and snakes.

How do caterpillars turn into butterflies?

A caterpillar starts its life by hatching from an egg. The caterpillar feeds and grows, and then wraps its body inside a hard case called a pupa. Next, the caterpillar completely changes shape in a process called metamorphosis. Finally, it leaves the pupa as an adult butterfly with wings.

3 Wrapping up
The pupa wraps around the caterpillar. Inside the pupa, the caterpillar's body starts to change shape.

2 Hanging on
When fully grown, the caterpillar attaches itself to a twig using a silken thread. It sheds its skin again and its new skin hardens into a tough case, called a pupa or chrysalis.

1 Eating leaves
A caterpillar, or butterfly larva, hatches from an egg. It eats mostly leaves and quickly outgrows its skin, which it sheds several times.

There are around **20,000 types** of butterfly in the world.

Quick quiz

★ What do caterpillars eat?

★ What happens inside the chrysalis?

★ Where do butterflies lay eggs?

Growing up

Many young insects, such as flies and beetles, look very different to fully-grown adults. Like caterpillars, they also start life as crawling larvae and turn into flying adults inside a hard case called a pupa.

Young fly larvae (or maggots)

Adult blue bottle fly

Young ladybird larvae

Adult ladybirds

4 Changing shape

The chrysalis changes colour as the caterpillar changes into a butterfly.

5 Splitting open

Finally, the chrysalis breaks open and the adult butterfly crawls out. Its large, crumpled wings have to expand and dry before it can fly.

Some butterflies fly 3,200 km (2,000 miles) to lay eggs.

6 Flying away

The butterfly flies away to visit flowers and feed on their sweet nectar. After mating, female butterflies lay their eggs on plants and the life cycle starts again!

Why do wasps sting?

Only female wasps and only some species of wasps can sting. Social wasps (which live in groups) may sting to defend themselves or their nests if they are in danger. Solitary wasps (which live alone) also use their sting to kill or stun their prey.

A sting in the tail......

A wasp's sting injects venom (poison) into its prey. Wasps can curl the back part of their body under and forwards to use the sting.

Insect defence

Not all insects have a sting to defend themselves. Assassin bugs can spit venom (poison) at an attacker from up to 30 cm (1 ft) away. They also kill prey by biting it and injecting it with venom. Sometimes they work as a team to overpower prey much bigger than themselves.

Assassin bug

Warning stripes.

These black and yellow stripes warn other animals that the wasp is dangerous.

Barbs and claws

Wasps have sharp barbs on their legs. At the end of their legs, claws help them to grip and carry prey.

Quick quiz

 Why do wasps have stripes?

 What are a wasp's antennae used for?

 How many lenses are in a wasp's eye?

A wasp can **sting many times**, but a bee can sting only once.

Scent detector
The stalks on a wasp's head are called antennae. It uses them to detect scents and tastes.

Super eyesight
A wasp's eyes are made up of thousands of tiny lenses. They make the wasp very good at spotting moving objects.

Pinching jaws
The wasp's jaws have hard, sharp edges. They work like scissors, pinching together to cut into and mash up prey.

Can anything survive in the desert?

Deserts are areas in which very little rain falls. Some are sandy and rocky places with little life. Others, such as the deserts of North America, get more rain, so more plants can grow there. Animals live in deserts, too. They have special ways of finding food and keeping cool in the burning heat.

Looking for food
The coyote feeds on fruit and insects – whatever it can find. It also hunts for small animals.

Globemallow

Jackrabbit

Tarantula

Storing water
Like many desert plants, the organ pipe cactus can store water inside its thick, waxy stems.

Giant ears
The jackrabbit's huge ears help it listen out for danger and also give off heat to help it stay cool.

Hunting at night
Rattlesnakes are expert hunters. They use heat sensors to find warm-blooded prey in the dark.

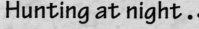

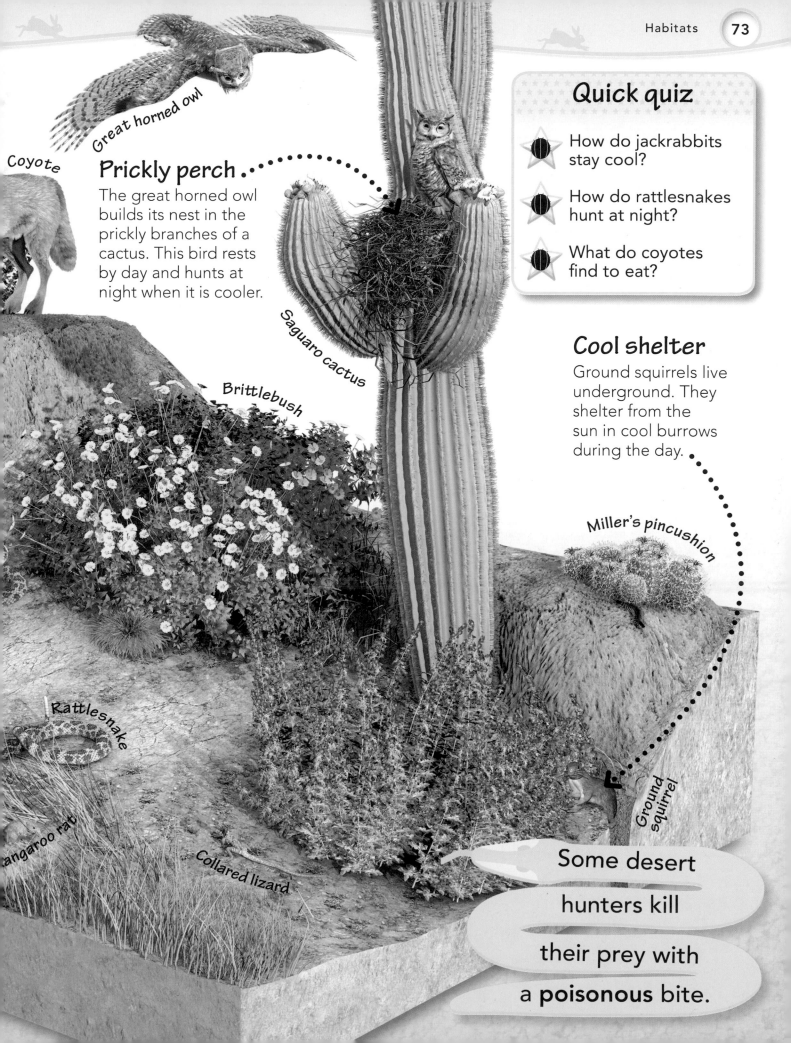

Great horned owl

Coyote

Prickly perch

The great horned owl builds its nest in the prickly branches of a cactus. This bird rests by day and hunts at night when it is cooler.

Saguaro cactus

Brittlebush

Rattlesnake

Kangaroo rat

Collared lizard

Cool shelter

Ground squirrels live underground. They shelter from the sun in cool burrows during the day.

Miller's pincushion

Ground squirrel

Some desert hunters kill their prey with a **poisonous** bite.

Vulture

Umbrella trees
They may be shaped like umbrellas, but acacia trees can live for months without rain.

Leading lion
The male lion is head of his family group, which is called a pride. He lets the lioness hunt for food, but is always first to eat.

Wildebeest

Cheetah

Do lions live in the jungle?

Lions don't live in the wet and steamy jungle (also known as a rainforest). They prefer the dry, open grasslands of Africa, which are called savannas. The savanna gets enough rain for shrubs and some trees to grow, and is home to many different kinds of animal.

A **lion's roar** can be heard up to **8 km (5 miles)** away.

Eating leftovers

Vultures are large birds that are scavengers. They eat the remains of the prey left behind by other animals.

The long trek

Many animals that live on the savanna, such as wildebeest, zebra, and gazelle, migrate at certain times of year. This means that they travel hundreds of kilometres seeking fresh grass for grazing.

Elephant

Vulture

Gazelle

Zebra

Water danger

While zebra drink at the water hole, they look out for danger. Lions, cheetahs, and leopards will lurk nearby, hunting for prey.

Quick quiz

- What is another name for a jungle?
- What is a family of lions called?
- Which trees look like umbrellas?

What is a rainforest?

A rainforest (also called a jungle) is a place where lots of different types of tree grow. Tropical rainforests have hot, humid, rainy weather all year round. More than half of all plant and animal species live in rainforests such as the Amazon in Brazil.

Scarlet macaw

Flying high
Colourful scarlet macaws, a kind of parrot, fly from tree to tree to feed on nuts and fruit.

Toucan

Top to bottom

A rainforest has different layers where animals live or find food. "Emergent trees" grow up above the main canopy (tree tops). They get bright sunlight, while the forest floor doesn't get much light at all.

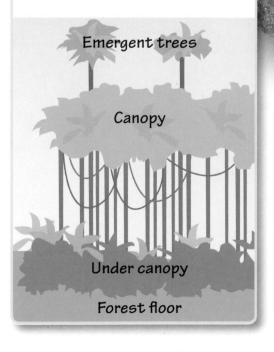

Emergent trees

Canopy

Under canopy

Forest floor

Piranha

Black caiman

Giant otter

Amazon river

Quick quiz

 What do scarlet macaws feed on?

 How does the emerald tree boa kill prey?

 Do jaguars always stay on the forest floor?

Swooping in

When a harpy eagle sees a monkey or sloth in the trees, it swoops down to grab it in its strong claws.

Harpy eagle

Monkeying around

Howler monkeys live in the canopy and feed on leaves. They wake up the rainforest at dawn with their loud howls.

Blue-and-yellow macaw

Howler monkey

Rainforests cover less than **6 per cent** of the Earth's surface.

Snakes alive

An emerald tree boa blends in among the green leaves. It squeezes its prey to death.

On the prowl

A jaguar roams the forest floor looking for prey. It can also climb trees and will even swim in the river.

Emerald tree boa

Capybara

Jaguar

Green iguana

Giant water lily

History

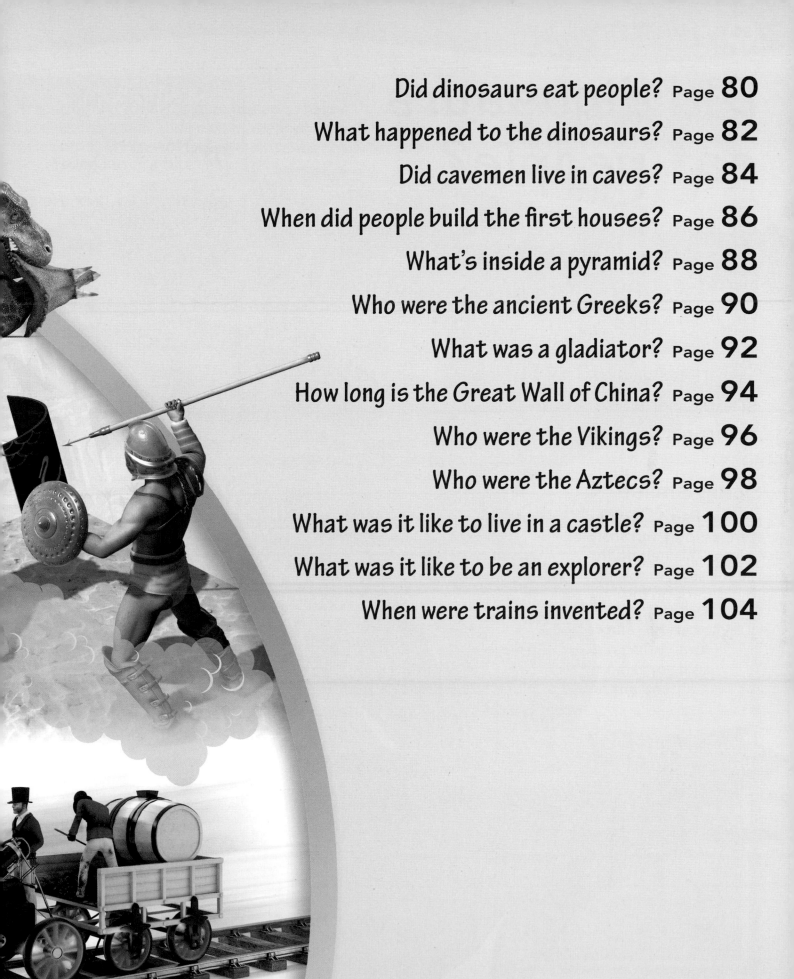

Did cavemen live in caves?

Tens of thousands of years ago, some early people used caves to shelter from the weather or to hide from wild animals. It's thought they mostly used caves for short periods, however, and did not settle in them.

Early people often used

Cave painting

We know about early people because the cave paintings they made showed important events in their lives. This painting was probably made by Cro-Magnon people in around 15,000 BCE.

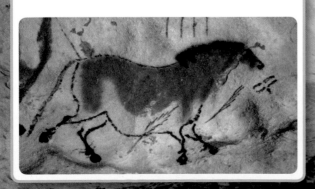

Room for one more

Most caves were only big enough for small groups. It's thought that Neanderthal people lived in groups of around 12 people.

caves while out hunting for food.

Early people

When people talk about cavemen, they often mean Neanderthals. This early form of human had a heavy build, which helped protect against cold weather. They died out around 30,000 years ago.

Several **different species of human ancestors** used caves for shelter.

What was a gladiator?

Two thousand years ago, in Roman cities, crowds gathered to be entertained by watching people fight. The fighters were called gladiators, and sometimes they fought to the death. There were more than 20 types of gladiator, which fought with different weapons.

Short sword

Some gladiators fought with a short, curved sword called a sica.

Animals, too!

Before the gladiators stepped into the arena, the crowds were entertained by trained hunters who would fight animals such as lions and wolves.

The **first gladiators** were **prisoners** from countries invaded by the Roman army.

Protecting the body...

A gladiator's shield was large and oblong, or small and round, depending on the weapon he carried.

... And the head

Headgear was made to be showy to impress people, as well as to provide good protection.

Sharp spear

Some gladiators used long spears to jab at their opponent. The spears were wooden poles, tipped with an iron point.

Quick quiz

 How many types of gladiator were there?

 Was a sica a spear or a sword?

 What did gladiators wear on their feet?

Gladiators fought on sand.

Mix and match

Gladiators often wore protective leg armour, but not everyone had the same armour or weapons. The crowds enjoyed seeing how the differences affected the fights.

No shoes!

Gladiators fought in bare feet or wore strappy leather sandals.

How long is the Great Wall of China?

Around 1,740 km (1,080 miles) of the Great Wall stands today, but no one really knows how far it stretched at its longest, 500 years ago. Estimates range from 8,850 km (5,500 miles) to more than 21,000 km (13,000 miles) in total.

Wide walls

The widest parts of the wall were 9 m (30 ft) across. At its narrowest, the wall was just 30 cm (12 in) wide – the length of a ruler).

The top of the Great Wall was used as a road.

Signal towers

Signal towers were built along the wall. Messages, such as warnings of invasions, were sent from one tower to another.

Where the wall was

This map shows where the wall was 500 years ago. At first, there were several short walls, which were built 2,800 years ago. They were joined up around 400 years later, and were added to over time.

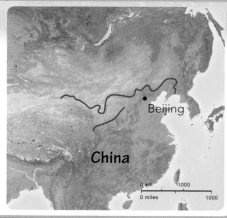

Beijing

China

0 km   1000
0 miles   1000

The first walls were built to **stop northern tribes** from **invading** farmland.

Alarm calls
A cannon was used to send loud warning signals if enemies were going to attack.

Smoke signals
Fires burned by the towers. They were used to send smoke signals during the day, to warn of attacks or to get help.

Quick quiz
- How much of the wall is standing today?
- Why were smoke signals sent?
- How many people built the wall?

On the look out
Soldiers guarded each section of the wall, looking out for invaders.

Lots of labour
It took hundreds of thousands of people to build the Great Wall.

What was it like to live in a castle?

A castle could be cold, damp, dark, smelly, and draughty. After all, it was built to keep enemies out, with huge outer walls, hefty corner towers, and narrow slits instead of windows.

Look out!

Towers at the corners of the castle allowed defenders to see if enemies were coming.

Living rooms

The lord's private rooms, called the solar, were in the strongest part of the castle.

Don't cross the water

A deep moat filled with water ran around the castle. It kept attackers away from the walls.

Raise the drawbridge

At the castle entrance, a wooden drawbridge could be lowered to let guests in, or raised to keep attackers out.

The way in

A castle had one main entrance, which made it easier to defend.

This is a **concentric castle** from the 13th century. It has two outer walls.

Fit for a feast

Inside the great hall, the lord would hold feasts for knights and guests.

Vegetable garden

Luxury living

The lord and his family lived and slept in the solar. He had a grand bed with a feather mattress, quilts, and fur covers – and linen curtains to keep draughts out.

Quick quiz

 What was the solar?

 What was a moat filled with?

 Where were feasts held?

Why do ice lollies melt?

When you take an ice lolly out of the freezer, it is solid. Solid objects are made of tiny particles (pieces) that are packed tightly together and don't move much. As the ice lolly warms up, it melts and turns into liquid. This happens because the heat gives the particles more energy and they spread out away from each other.

Frozen solid

A solid ice lolly has a definite shape.

Free flowing

The melted ice has turned into a liquid, which does not have a definite shape. The liquid flows (moves) to fill the space it is in.

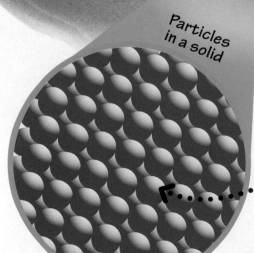

Particles in a solid

On the spot

The particles in a solid do not have enough energy to move around. They vibrate (jiggle) slightly, but not enough for you to see.

Quick quiz

 Do the particles in a frozen ice lolly move?

 Does a liquid have a definite shape?

 At what temperature does water freeze?

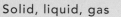

From liquid to gas

Water is a liquid, but it can be changed into a solid or a gas. When water is frozen, it turns into ice, which is a solid. When water is heated, it turns into steam, which is a gas. The particles in a gas move even faster than in a liquid and spread out in all directions.

Particles in a gas

Particles in a liquid

 **Breaking away**

As the ice lolly warms up in the air, the particles inside the ice gain more energy. This allows them to break away from each other and move around freely.

Water freezes into ice at 0°C (32°F) and boils to become steam at 100°C (212°F).

Why does metal get rusty?

Only iron and metals that contain iron, such as steel, get rusty. Iron rusts when it comes into contact with water and air. This is because the water and oxygen in the air react with the iron. This reaction create a new substance – the reddish-brown flakes of rust.

Quick quiz

 What kind of metal goes rusty?

 What are bicycle tyres made from?

 Which parts of a bicycle can rust?

Rustless rubber

Bicycle tyres will not rust because they are made of rubber. Rubber does not react with oxygen in the way that iron does.

Chain reaction

A bicycle chain is made of steel, so it will rust. You can prevent rust by putting oil on the chain, which helps to keep water off it.

In the saddle

A bicycle seat made of leather or plastic will not rust, but it might get torn or wear out.

Painting iron can keep it from rusting, because paint helps to **keep out air and water.**

Rusty chips

A bicycle frame is also made of steel and will go rusty if the metal is in contact with air and water for a long time. The frame is protected by paint, but if the paint is chipped, rust will form on the metal underneath.

Materials in your home

"Materials" is a word for the different stuff that things are made from, such as metal, plastic, or glass. Your home is full of objects made from different materials.

Plastic
Toy

Glass
Drinking glass

Wood
Chair

Wool
Jumper

Metal
Knife and fork

What is energy?

Energy is the ability to do work. Work can include many things such as walking to school, turning the wheels of a car, powering a computer, or making plants and animals grow. Most of the energy on the Earth comes from the Sun.

Energy cannot be **created** or **destroyed.** It simply **changes** from one form to another.

1 Heat and light

Nuclear reactions inside the Sun change matter into light energy and heat energy. This energy travels through space to the Earth.

2 Growing plants

Plants such as wheat take in the Sun's energy and use it to make sugars. The wheat stores the energy from the sugars inside its cells and uses it for growth

Ready to go

When you stretch a rubber band, you use some energy. The band stores this energy for as long as you hold it. If you let it go suddenly, the rubber band then changes the stored energy into kinetic (movement) energy and sound energy, as it moves with a "boing".

3 Eating food

Bread contains the stored energy from the wheat. When we eat it, or any other food, our bodies store the energy from the food and use it to power everything from our brains to our muscles.

Quick quiz

 Where does energy come from?

 What do plants use energy for?

 Can energy be destroyed?

4 On the move

When we run, the energy stored in our bodies changes into kinetic (movement) energy. If we kick a ball, some of this energy is passed on to the ball, making it move.

Where does electricity come from?

Most of the electricity people use in their homes comes from a power plant. The electricity travels along power lines to our homes, where we use it for cooking, heating, lighting, and running appliances such as televisions.

❸ On the move
The high-voltage electricity is carried along power lines supported by huge towers called pylons.

❷ Step up
The electricity travels to a "step-up" substation, which increases the electricity's voltage (pressure that pushes it along). This makes it easier to move and wastes less energy.

Fossil fuels are formed underground from the remains of ancient plants and animals.

❶ Power plant
At most power stations, fossil fuels such as coal, oil, or gas are burned to heat water to make steam. This steam turns a wheel called a turbine to make electricity.

Quick quiz

 Can you name three fossil fuels?

 What happens in a power plant?

 Why is solar power a renewable energy source?

5 Coming home

The lower-voltage electricity is carried along another set of power lines and pylons to the power sockets in people's homes.

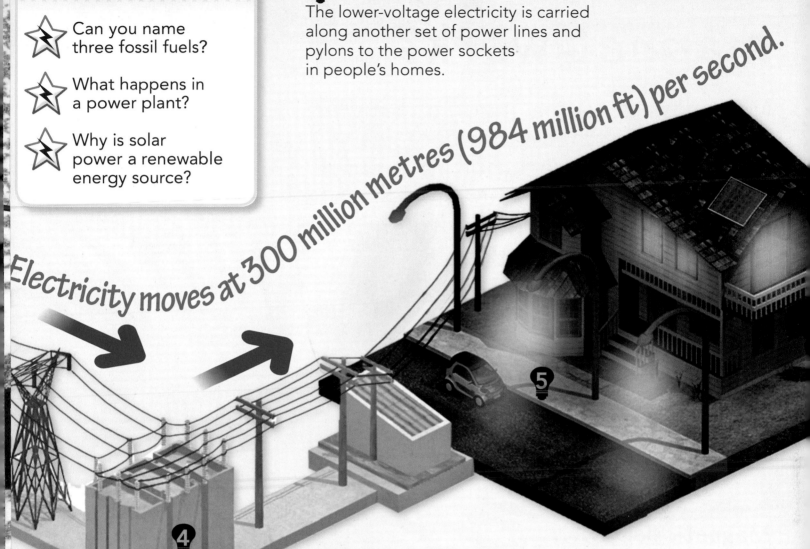

Electricity moves at 300 million metres (984 million ft) per second.

4 Step down

The electricity reaches another substation, where the electricity's voltage is reduced. This makes it safer to use in people's homes.

Energy forever

Fossil fuels are a non-renewable source of energy: there is a fixed amount of them on the Earth and they may all be used up one day. However, there are also renewable energy sources. The power of the wind, water, or the Sun will never run out.

Hydroelectric power uses water moving through a dam to create electricity.

Wind power uses the wind to turn huge turbines, which produce electricity.

Solar power turns light from the Sun's rays into electricity.

What makes a car go?

Most cars are powered by an engine that uses petrol or diesel, which are liquid fuels. The car's engine burns this fuel to move a system of rods and cogs, which turn the car's wheels and make it go.

Electric cars don't use petrol, but run on **battery power** using an **electric motor.**

Reverse gear turns the wheels backwards.

Quick quiz

 Which fuels power most cars?

 What does a gearbox do?

 What does a drive shaft connect to?

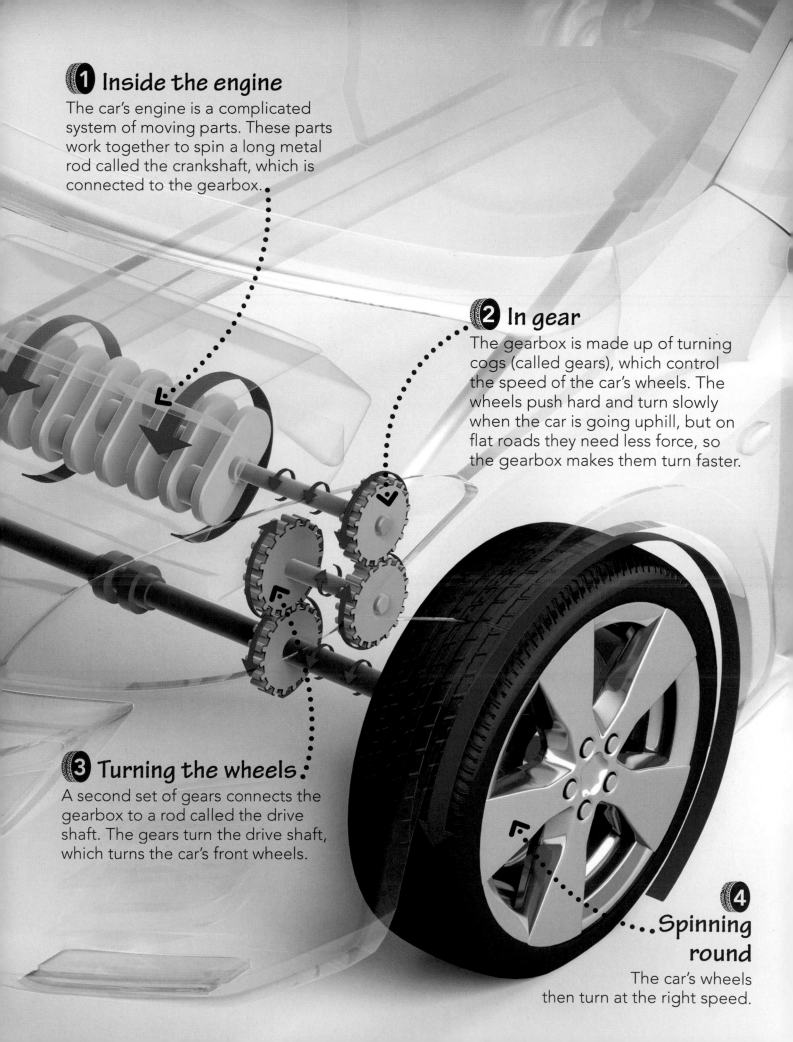

1 Inside the engine

The car's engine is a complicated system of moving parts. These parts work together to spin a long metal rod called the crankshaft, which is connected to the gearbox.

2 In gear

The gearbox is made up of turning cogs (called gears), which control the speed of the car's wheels. The wheels push hard and turn slowly when the car is going uphill, but on flat roads they need less force, so the gearbox makes them turn faster.

3 Turning the wheels

A second set of gears connects the gearbox to a rod called the drive shaft. The gears turn the drive shaft, which turns the car's front wheels.

4 ...Spinning round

The car's wheels then turn at the right speed.

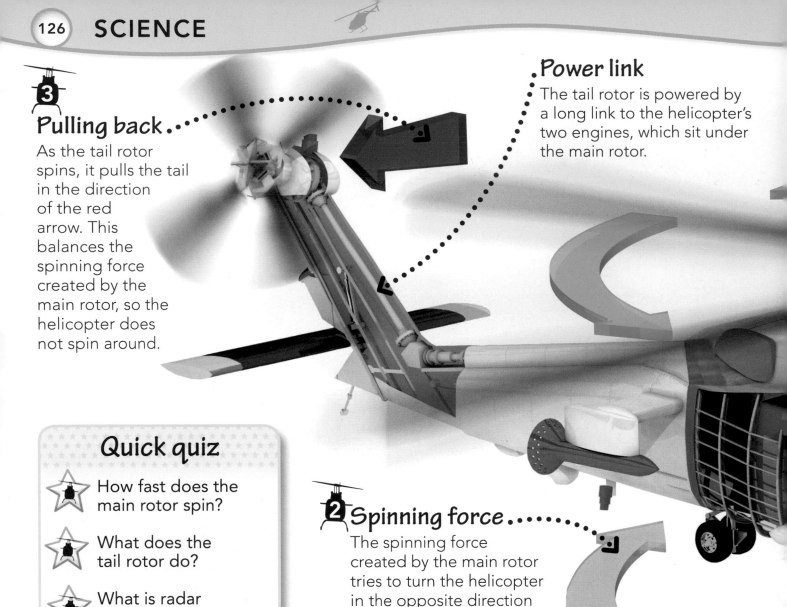

3 Pulling back

As the tail rotor spins, it pulls the tail in the direction of the red arrow. This balances the spinning force created by the main rotor, so the helicopter does not spin around.

Power link

The tail rotor is powered by a long link to the helicopter's two engines, which sit under the main rotor.

2 Spinning force

The spinning force created by the main rotor tries to turn the helicopter in the opposite direction to the rotor (shown by the orange arrows).

Quick quiz

★ How fast does the main rotor spin?

★ What does the tail rotor do?

★ What is radar used for?

Why does a helicopter have a propeller on its tail?

The propellers are actually called rotors, and most helicopters have two of them – the main rotor and the tail rotor. The main rotor lifts the helicopter off the ground, but it also creates a spinning force that tries to spin the whole helicopter around. The tail rotor's job is to stop that happening.

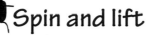

1 Spin and lift

The main rotor turns hundreds of times every minute, in the direction of the green arrows. This creates a force called lift, which raises the helicopter into the sky.

Search equipment

Radar, satellite navigation, and night-vision equipment are used to search for objects, especially at sea.

Rescue service

This search-and-rescue helicopter has a stretcher that can be lowered to pick up injured people.

Taking control

The pilot flies the helicopter by using two separate hand controls and two foot controls.

A helicopter can fly **up**, **down**, **forwards**, **sideways**, **backwards**, and even **hover in one place**.

Twin rotor Chinook

The Chinook helicopter has two main rotors, but no tail rotor. The main rotors turn in opposite directions. One tries to spin the helicopter one way, while the other does the opposite. They balance each other out, so no tail rotor is needed.

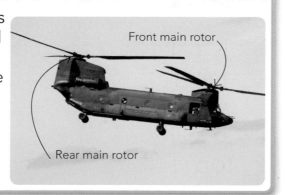

Front main rotor

Rear main rotor

How do mobile phones work?

When a person sends a text, their mobile phone sends it as invisible radio waves to a tower called a base station. There are lots of base stations, which are connected by computers inside a building called a switching office. These computers pass the message on from one base station to another, and then on to the phone being called.

Radio waves

First base station

The **first text message** was sent in 1992 in the UK. It said, "Merry Christmas".

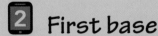

1 Press send

When a text message is sent, the phone sends the message through the air as invisible radio waves. These are picked up by the nearest base station (a special tower with an antenna on top).

2 First base

The base station receives the radio waves and sends them as an electronic signal along an underground cable to a network of computers inside a building called a switching office.

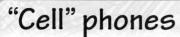

"Cell" phones

Base stations are spread out across a country. Each base station stands in its own area, which is called a cell. This is why, in many countries, mobile phones are called cell phones.

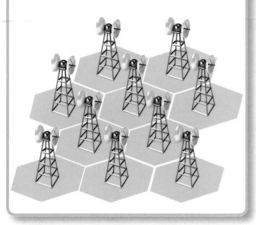

Quick quiz

 What does a phone send to a base station?

 What did the first text message say?

 How many base stations are in a cell?

Second base station

Radio waves

Switching office

HELLO

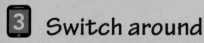

 3 Switch around

The computers in the switching office find the base station nearest to the phone that the text is being sent to. It then passes the signal along cables to this base station.

4 Second base

The second base station receives the signal, turns it back into radio waves, and sends them through the air to the phone.

 5 Message received!

The phone picks up the radio waves and changes them back into the original message.

How many bones are there in my body?

The human body contains 206 bones. More than half of these are in your hands and feet. Bones make up a frame for your body, called a skeleton. They also work with your muscles to help you move, and protect your organs.

Hinged at the knees

The place where two bones meet is called a joint. The knee is the largest joint in your body and bends like a hinge.

One-sixth of your body weight is bone.

Thigh bone (femur)

Shin bone (tibia)

Hip bone (pelvis)

Flexible foot

There are 26 bones in each foot. This helps to make them flexible enough for walking, jumping, and running.

Quick quiz

 What is the largest joint in your body?

 Is the skull one bone or many bones?

 How many bones make up the spine?

Super skull

The skull is made up of 22 bones, though most of these are locked together. In fact, only the lower jaw can move.

Elbow joint

The elbow is a hinge joint, like the knee. It lets you bend and straighten your arm.

Arm bone (radius)

Collar bone (clavicle)

Protective cage

Your ribs form a cage that protects the soft, delicate organs inside your body, such as your heart and lungs.

Bendy backbone

The backbone, or spine, is made up of 24 bones called vertebrae. These help you to twist and bend.

Bone is **six times stronger** than a steel bar of the same weight.

Growing bones

A baby's skeleton is mostly cartilage – the same stuff your ears are made from. Unlike your ears, however, this cartilage stiffens into bone as a child grows.

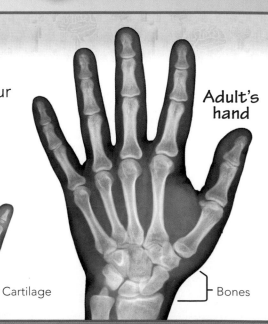

Adult's hand

Infant's hand

Cartilage

Bones

Biggest bone

The thigh bone is the strongest and heaviest bone in your body. It is also the longest – a quarter of your height.

At the elbow

The movement of your elbow (the joint where your arm bones meet) is controlled by a pair of muscles called the biceps and triceps.

 Bending

When your biceps muscle contracts (gets shorter and thicker), it bends your elbow and pulls your lower arm towards your shoulder.

Biceps

Triceps

Why do I have muscles?

Muscles are important because they help your body to move. Without them, you would not be able to walk, jump, blink, or breathe. Muscles are made of bundles of fibres, each one as thin as a hair.

Your **biggest muscle** is in your bottom. It is called the **gluteus maximus**.

Tough tendons

Your muscles are attached to your bones by tendons. They look like thin cords, and are very strong.

❷ Straightening

When your triceps muscle contracts (gets shorter and thicker), it pulls your lower arm away from your shoulder.

Biceps

Pull-not-push pairs

Your body has more than 640 muscles that help you move. Like your biceps and triceps, these muscles can pull but cannot push, so they work in pairs that pull in opposite directions. For example, to move your foot, a muscle in your shin pulls it up, while a muscle at the back of your calf pulls it back down again.

Muscle pulls foot down

Muscle pulls foot up

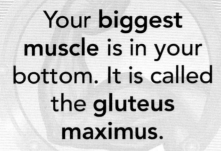

How do my eyes work?

When you look at an object, light bounces off it and enters your eye. The eye turns this into a signal that it sends to your brain. Your brain then tells you what you are looking at.

Eye colour
The coloured disc at the front of your eyeball is called the iris. It controls how much light gets in.

Light rays
When you look at an object, light rays bounce off that object and enter your eye.

Black hole
In the centre of your iris is a tiny hole called the pupil, which looks black. The pupil lets light into your eye. It gets bigger in the dark to help you see more.

Into focus
The transparent lens changes shape, to let you see things that are near and far away.

It is impossible to **sneeze** with your **eyes open.**

Just jelly!

Your eye is a squashy ball filled with a jelly-like liquid. This liquid helps it to keep its round shape.

Light detection

The retina is a layer of light-sensitive cells at the back of your eye. When light hits the cells, they send messages to your brain.

Topsy turvy

The lens bends the light so everything we see is upside down. Our brain turns it the right way round again.

Roll your eyes

Six muscles move your eyeball, so you can look from side to side and up and down.

To the brain

Your optic nerve carries light signals to your brain.

Your five senses

Humans have five senses: sight, hearing, smell, touch, and taste. Senses work together to help you understand the world.

See

Hear

Smell

Touch

Taste

Quick quiz

 What is the coloured part of your eye called?

 Where is your pupil?

 How do light signals reach your brain?

Why do I sneeze?

Sneezing helps your body to get rid of something it doesn't want inside it. If you breathe in tiny grains of dust or plant pollen, they tickle the inside of your nose, making you sneeze them out. Cold germs also make you sneeze, but sneezing out the germs can pass them on to other people.

Dirt catchers

Tiny hairs in your nose help catch grains of dirt that you breathe in, so they do not enter your lungs.

Speedy sneezing

When you sneeze, the mucus droplets fly out at speeds of up to 40 kph (25 mph). That's as fast as sprinter Usain Bolt can run!

Washing hands

If you sneeze out the cold virus, it can live for hours on many objects that people touch, such as door handles, phones, and skin. Washing your hands helps to get rid of the virus and keep you healthy.

The world's longest ever sneezing fit lasted 978 days!

Sneezing uses muscles in your tummy, chest, nose, and throat.

Quick quiz

 Name two things that make you sneeze.

 What are the hairs in your nose for?

 What does mucus contain?

At-choo!

The droplets you sneeze out are called mucus. If you have a cold and other people breathe in your mucus, they can catch your cold.

Pollen grain

Pollen grain

Bacteria

Pollen grain

Dust

Cold virus

Dust

Inside the droplets

Each droplet can contain many different things, including living things. This picture magnifies them thousands of times.